Kingdom Seeker's Devotional

Searching the Deep Things of God

By Krista Dunk
©2015

Kingdom Seeker's Devotional
© 2015 by Krista Dunk
www.KristaDunk.com

This title is also available as an eBook. Visit www.CreativeForcePress.com/titles for more information.

Published by Creative Force Press
4704 Pacific Ave, Suite C, Lacey, WA 98503
www.CreativeForcePress.com

Scripture taken from the New King James Version®. Copyright © 1982 by Thomas Nelson, Inc. Used by permission. All rights reserved.

All rights reserved. No part of this publication may be reproduced, stored in a retrieval system, or transmitted in any form or by any means--for example, electronic, photocopy, recording--without the prior written permission of the publisher.

ISBN: 978-1-939989-16-1

Printed in the United States of America

Dedication

To every one of God's people who are unsatisfied with less than obtaining **all** spiritual blessings available to them in Christ.

We desire You, Father of Lights.

To my husband and children, who God will use to minister to others in powerful ways.

Contents

Preface	9
I Am Earth	11
Heaven on Earth	13
Enough	15
Jesus Defeated That	17
It's Your Choice	19
Impartation	21
Prayer of Revival	23
Win-Win	24
Keep Listening	25
Family Issues	27
Every Word	29
Temptation Trinity	31
7 Lessons of Temptation	33
Power Supply	35
They've Got Nothing	37
Longing for Perfection	39
He is Everything	41
Habits or Faith?	43
39%	45
Bad Breath	47
Righteousness	49
The Key	51
External Viewpoint	53
Bondage to Prosperity	55
Illegal Substance	57
Praise Emission	59
Keep Your Harvest	61
Say Something	63

Kingdom Currency	65
Desolate Heritages	68
Get His Vision	71
The Cross of 'Others'	73
Keep it Simple	75
Disappointments	77
Release Your Words!	79
Survival Mode	81
Kingdom Increase	83
Wind, Fire and Oil	86
Hands and Mouths	89
Lord, I'm Distressed	91
Legal System	93
Strongholds	95
Quotes and Thoughts	98
About the Author	99

Preface

There is more. More, much more to know about God and His Kingdom, no matter how long we've been saved. More layers of truth to be discovered in each scripture verse, underneath the obvious meaning. More experiences, visions and access available, but only for the hungry.

These devotionals come directly from my time spent in prayer, study and quiet time seeking God. My journals filled with questions, answers and new understanding are some of my most precious and valuable possessions.

Several years ago, I made a promise to God. My promise was that whatever He spoke, revealed or showed to me, that I would then carry it forward and share it with others as He directs. This book is a part of keeping that promise.

I pray that you'll be blessed by these devotions. Some may leave you with more questions. Some may answer questions you've had.

My hope is that you'll get a vision and *see* it; see and understand the truths with your spiritual eyes and imagination, not just with logic. Jesus always taught hoping people would see past the obvious, natural implications and understand deeper, spiritual things.

May we have eyes that see and ears that hear.

Krista Dunk, 2015

I Am Earth

"And the Lord God formed man of the dust of the ground, and breathed into his nostrils the breath of life; and man became a living being." –Genesis 2:7

God made Adam in His image to be in charge of this domain: earth. Known in Hebrew as *Adamah*, his name means soil, field, red, dirt; made of the very substance of the planet he was meant to have dominion over.

We, as spiritual, earthly beings, contain all of the elements. We are earth, wind, water, and fire.

Earth – We were formed of the soil.
Wind – God breathed His breath into us.
Water – Our bodies are largely made up of water.
Fire – We were designed to contain the Holy Spirit.

Interestingly, both our bodies and the surface of the earth are approximately 70% water. Coincidence? I don't think so.

"But the ones that fell on the good ground are those who, having heard the word with a noble and good heart, keep it and bear fruit with patience." –Luke 8:15

*"...if My people who are called by My name will humble themselves, and pray and seek My face, and turn from their wicked ways, then I will hear from heaven, and will forgive their sin and heal their **land**."* –2 Chronicles 7:14

Could the *land* that needs to be healed...be us? Consider that whenever the Bible mentions land, earth or a field in the Bible, there is a deeper reference. God may be referring to you and me.

"So shall my word be that goes forth from My mouth; it shall not return to Me void, but it shall accomplish what I please, and it shall prosper in the thing for which I sent it." –Isaiah 55:11

From the beginning, God always intended for us to be the field in which He wants to plant. He sends His Word, which is powerful, spiritual seed, to settle into our hearts and produce its fruit; fruit that remains.

His Word was always meant to grow more Kingdom.

As the very material this planet is made of, the spiritual kingdoms of light and darkness need our authorization and cooperation to be at work here. Which kingdom will you serve and increase the influence of?

Genesis 2
John 15:16

Heaven on Earth

"Our Father in heaven, hallowed be Your name. Your kingdom come. Your will be done on earth as it is in heaven. Give us day by day our daily bread. And forgive us our sins, for we also forgive everyone who is indebted to us. And do not lead us into temptation, but deliver us from the evil one."
–Luke 11:2-4

As people who trust in the name of Jesus and have the deposit of the Holy Spirit, Heaven is our eternal home. Today, while living on earth, we are having a mid-range experience, influenced by both light and darkness. The only reason there is any good, love and joy in the world is because God's Kingdom of light is at work. The only reason there is evil and pain is because Satan's kingdom is also at work.

In Heaven, there is only light and fullness of joy; only good, blessing, love, peace, safety, rest, strength, truth, beauty, and perfection. Imagine this astounding place: streets of gold, trees that continuously produce fruit and instantly replace fruit that has been eaten, dwellings for each person designed specifically for them, beauty and colors like we've never seen before, the River of Life flowing from God Himself and splitting into many waterways, angels mingling freely with people, full wisdom and understanding of truths, reuniting with missed loved ones and friends, brilliant music like we've never heard, and talking to Jesus face-to-face.

There is no sickness, no disease, no pain, no poverty, no fear, nothing dangerous, no boredom, no depression, no worry, no confusion, no loneliness, nothing rotten, no garbage, no pollution, and zero temptation to sin.

When we pray "Thy Kingdom come on earth (here)," we ask the Lord to make the realities of Heaven happen here, *now*; in our bodies, homes, finances, relationships, situations, surroundings, wisdom and revelation, heavenly hosts' help, etc. All that He has in Heaven is available to His children right now if we can only realize it. I've even heard He has a body parts room; a room full of new eyes of all colors, organs, tissues, teeth, knees, hearts, and more.

The Garden of Eden was, quite literally, a piece of Heaven on Earth. God wants us to authorize it to come again, today, bringing all its resources, peace and power.

I authorize all of Heaven's glory to come and be established in my life today! Yes, Your Kingdom expand and manifest in tangible ways on this earth…and since I am made of earth and Heaven, Your Kingdom come to this earth, Lord!

Isaiah 49:8
Hebrews 12:18-21

Enough

When everything is stripped away, is the Lord enough?

As I sat staring out across our nicely groomed property, watching birds flit in the trees, thankful in my heart for all of the Lord's blessings, yet silently admitting prideful thoughts that have crossed my mind, His Spirit asked a simple question:

"If you had nothing else but Me – this home, successes and accomplishments, cars, bank accounts, and material possessions the world finds valuable…gone – would you still consider yourself a rich woman?"

Stricken by the rawness of His question, I had no immediate answer for Him. The world tells us that 'rich' looks a certain way. From Heaven's perspective, 'rich' looks *very* different. I knew His question already had the correct answer built into it. Contemplating His wise inquiry and the full reality of it brought a clear understanding of its truth. He was teaching me to live with an open hand; to have a humble dependence on Him alone for all that my soul requires.

He wanted me to know that He is all I require.

Even Jesus had no regard for stuff or status to validate the immeasurable expanse of His true, Kingdom riches. The fullness of the Father was all He needed.

"Then a certain scribe came and said to Him, 'Teacher, I will follow You wherever You go.' And Jesus said to him, 'Foxes have holes and birds of the air have nests, but the Son of Man has nowhere to lay His head." – Matthew 8:20

To follow Him, means turning our eyes — even away from blessings He has given — to Him alone as our treasure.

If all I had was Jesus, I would have everything.

Jeremiah 9:23-24
Luke 16:11
Romans 12:3
Philippians 4:19
1 Timothy 6:17

Jesus Defeated That

You never know what someone is dealing with underneath the surface of their conversational small talk. One day, I sat with a young woman in a women's ministry discussion group. Our group had been in discussion for nearly an hour after hearing a short teaching. I had no idea this woman was struggling, until I asked, "Does anyone have any prayer requests?" As tears started to flow, she revealed that her mother had just been diagnosed with an aggressive cancer.

After she gave a few details, despair showing on her face, a thought for her rose up within my heart:

JESUS DEFEATED CANCER

Later that day, the unfolding of Jesus' complete victory exploded in my spirit. Jesus not only defeated cancer, but all sickness, disease and malady of every kind. Addictions and bondage were defeated. Poverty and lack were fully defeated. Depression and brokenheartedness...defeated. All sin, defeated. Even death itself was defeated. Chaos, confusion and every plot of darkness was defeated because of Jesus' work. It is finished!

This realization was powerful, but a question remained in my heart. *Jesus, if You have defeated these things, why do Your people still deal with issues You've already defeated?*

He answered: *Many have accepted bondages, lack and disease as if they are My will. Others do not have the knowledge of My victory over their circumstance, or of My willingness to heal, provide and deliver. Some are too afraid to be disappointed by not seeing an instant change that they never truly ask for My help. Most depend on their own understanding of natural things and man's wisdom, which cannot save. They see My help coming to them in Heaven after they die rather than in the land of the living, now.*

"*Jesus said to him, 'Thomas, because you have seen Me, you have believed. Blessed are those who have not seen and yet have believed.'*" –John 20:29

If deep in our hearts, we can truly believe Jesus is the Son of God, not having seen with our eyes, Lord likewise help us to believe *every* word You say with the same fullness of confident faith!

Jesus, what struggles remain in my life that You have defeated?

Isaiah 53:4-6
Isaiah 61:1-3
John 19:28-30

It's Your Choice

"Living in My presence is your choice."

Yes Lord, You are right. It is my choice. Your presence is ever with me; in me, in fact.

With the desperate cry of, "We need Your presence, Lord!" comes Your honest reply that the ball is in our court. Sometimes we ignore You for days, then wonder why we feel dry and desolate. All the while, You wait.

Walking in Your presence continuously, Ever-Faithful One, seems just out of reach. But Jesus did it, so we know it *is* possible. But how?

Lord, teach us how to engage Your presence; Your presence that is shammah – always there. YHWH Shammah – the Lord is there.

The reality that You are here, now, always, needs to take over. We don't need to beg You to come down or to come near, as if You are somewhere far away.

I understand that You inhabit the praises of Your people, and You draw near when we pray and worship.

"Call to Me, and I will answer you, and show you great and mighty things, which you do not know." –Jeremiah 33:3

Only I set the limits on how often we commune and how much I engage Your presence. That is the key – to *engage* Your presence. Living in Your presence *is* my choice. Teach me, Lord.

Psalm 16:11
Acts 2:28

Impartation

Intimacy leaves a deposit. All intimate relationships have a secret place; a place where doors are closed, shades are pulled and union takes place.

Intimacy with the Lord has to do with communion: a partaking in communication union and oneness. As we commune with Him, Jesus changes us by imparting something of Himself into us. Our spiritual hearts are His planting ground. Just as sexual intimacy can plant a seed and grow new life, so does God's Word and Spirit's planting grow new life.

Impartation, a transfer, happens during intimacy. God's cloud of glory is also an environment for impartation. The glory cloud is His manifest presence coming in a group setting, accompanied by His miracles, signs and wonders. Many seek after this experience at conferences and revival meetings, but may neglect the one-on-one, secret place time of preparation.

God brings His cloud of glory in group settings where individuals have spent time in the secret place with Him. They are ready, individually, for the corporate manifestation of His presence.

In the Garden of Eden, Adam and Eve had intimacy with the Lord. He walked with them. They were uncovered (naked) and not ashamed; completely open to Him with no barrier. Until...sin. Suddenly, they felt a great need for a covering; something to put on to buffer and hide their bare selves from His eyes. Their intimacy became guarded.

As a picture of Jesus, God clothed Adam and Eve with a sacrifice.

Today, Jesus is our covering. He is the head and the covering for His body. Because of the Holy Spirit, intimacy has been restored. How much intimacy we experience and how unguarded we are with God is purely our decision.

May we, as His body, experience personal intimacy with God and corporate glory. This is one of God's greatest desires.

*"Behold, I stand at the door and knock. If anyone hears My voice and opens the door, I will come **in to** him and dine with him, and he with Me."* –Revelation 3:20

Genesis 2
John 17

Prayer of Revival

Lord, let your fire of revival and of the Holy Spirit spread like wildfire! Let it come to this family, to this city, to this nation, to Your church. May it completely transform our government and politics, our modes of entertainment, our educational systems, and our priorities as a people.

May every tongue that rises against Your church be cut down and anything spoken against us not even be believed because we've become people of such high integrity, love and power.

We need a good house cleaning, Father – the house of God needs cleansing, purity and holiness more than ever. Wash us, Lord, and may the light of Your presence expose and chase away anything and everything not of Your Kingdom within us.

In Jesus' name, amen.

Win-Win

"But seek first the kingdom of God and His righteousness, and all these things shall be added to you."
–Matthew 6:33

As a businessperson, I often look for the 'win-win' in every endeavor. What I'm doing is a win for me and also for the person I'm working with. Even better is the triple win; the win-win-win situation (when three parties are involved). This has been my objective when serving and working with others. Until...

While praying about an opportunity recently, God made it clear to me that there is an additional 'win' I have to take into consideration: *His Kingdom must also win.*

When partnering, it must be a win for me, for the partner, for the people we serve, AND for God's Kingdom for it to be right. If the Kingdom doesn't clearly win in some way, it's not something for me to participate in.

A 3-way win is very good, but the optimum deal, situation or decision considers if the Kingdom will win, too.

Keep Listening

"I have more to say."

Often in my quiet time with the Lord, I will ask, "What else?" after He has shown or spoken something to me. There are always more details; always additional understanding He has to share.

A new perspective dawned on me one day: What He said in the Bible is not all He has to say. This could seem controversial to some, but let me explain.

The Lord, in the Bible, had prophetic revelation — or a 'proceeding word' — specifically to say to individuals, families, people groups, nations, etc. Can we accurately think He is done speaking to individuals, families, people groups, and nations of our day? No, He has more to say.

First and foremost, all that He would say today must align with written biblical truths. Reading the Bible helps us plant His Word in our hearts, and it also helps us to know Him, His character, and His heart so He can speak a *now* word to us and we'll recognize His voice. Without having the written Word stored up in our hearts, we could easily be deceived by any 'spiritual' voice that speaks to us.

Does God speak to us today through what is written in His Word? Definitely, yes! Does God speak to us today through His Holy Spirit as we spend time in His presence in prayer, study and worship? Yes. Does God speak through images in our imagination, cause us to recognize His hand in something, and give us understanding through natural circumstances and processes? Also, yes. Do not put limits on how God speaks. The antichrist spirit would attempt to silence His *now* voice and tell you He has nothing more to say.

If you're thinking, *I don't know how to hear what God has to say to me. He hasn't individually spoken to me.* Let me encourage you! God *has* spoken to you and God *has* directed you; you just may not have recognized it, yet.

> *"Call to Me, and I will answer you, and show you great and mighty things, which you do not know."* –Jeremiah 33:3

The Bible doesn't specifically tell you things like who to marry, what your calling is in life according to His unique design for you, or where to live. However, does the Lord have something to say to you regarding these important, current life issues? YES! Keep storing His Word in your heart so He can build upon it. Keep practicing being still and listening.

Listen and watch for what He wants to say, today.

John 16

Family Issues

"I have given you family so you will understand My heart for My church; for My children – the love, the dreams I have for them as a Father, the turmoil I experience, the deep concern, the joy I experience, the responsibility each one has, the variety and diversity of each individual, the power of unity and the weakness of division, My fierce loyalty, how to love imperfection, and an opportunity to practice forgiveness and the fruit of the Spirit."

Much of the forgiveness, grace, longsuffering, and love we need to offer or endure in life is due to our family relationships. They are deeper; they hit the core of who we are. We have higher expectations of family, and a greater correlation to our own identity wrapped up in them. To a degree, they are us and we are them.

Family is our first spiritual training ground, and continues to be the main training ground throughout our lives. If we are failing at family, as individuals and/or as a unit, that is a good indication that we don't have fruit of the Spirit that remains. Are we deceiving ourselves about how spiritual we really are?

In all transparency, do I find it easier to launch out and minister to others outside of my family, or is that harder? Or, does 'launching in' and taking good spiritual and emotional care of my family seem easier, or harder? But within that determination, does 'easier' equate to which group is easiest to control or manage?

Family is a blessing. As God's people, we are His family. Within family, there are issues. Thankfully, He is a perfect Father, and we can trust His judgment and love. When we understand our Father's blueprint for family, we understand His heart for His church.

Have I done all I can to launch in and love?

Every Word

Jesus chooses His words wisely. Even so, Jesus says things I don't always understand. Things we don't understand are more difficult to believe.

Pharisees often took time to listen to Jesus' teaching but did not accept His wisdom. On one occasion, a paralyzed man was lowered down on a bed through the roof of a packed house. After seeing this act of great faith, Jesus said, *"Man, your sins are forgiven you."*

The internal conversation of the Pharisees and scribes immediately refuted Jesus' words. *Who does this guy think he is?*

Knowing their thoughts, Jesus answered them with a question: *"Why are you reasoning in your hearts?"*

It's a puzzling question; one that He still asks those of us who hear His Word today. He speaks difficult truths and surprising revelation to us at times – *Wow, Lord, I didn't know* – but our ability to reason was never meant to doubt His words.

Why do we allow ourselves to take what the Lord says and process it through our belief systems; to evaluate it according to our own understanding? Is *my* logic a proper filter for the Creator of the universe's wisdom and truths? Why do I reason His truths away in my heart? Who do I think I am? Internal reasoning may sound like this:

- *I haven't personally experienced that aspect of His Word so it must not be real, or for believers today.*
- *I haven't seen it happen with my own eyes so I can't believe it. [Doubting Thomas]*
- *That doesn't make sense to me – I can't see or understand it, therefore I'm dismissing it.*
- *That goes against what a person taught me; against human wisdom, so it must not be right.*

A concrete path cannot receive a seed. Be careful – certain types of Word seeds may fall on uninhabitable, impenetrable ground in our hearts.

It seems like a waste of time to listen to the teachings of Jesus and not accept or believe them. Why bother? If He is God, serve Him!

Lord, my belief systems do not exist to evaluate what You say for correctness or believability. Help me believe every word You say. Amen.

Luke 5:17-26

Temptation Trinity

"Then Jesus was led up by the Spirit into the wilderness to be tempted by the devil. And when He had fasted forty days and forty nights, afterward He was hungry." –Matthew 4:1-2

Temptation…more than the off-limits cookie jar at grandma's house or a forbidden kiss. Satan has a specific strategy to ensnare humanity: it's a temptation trinity.

We are triune beings just like God; we have a body, soul and spirit. Satan has specific kinds of temptations cleverly designed to ensnare each part of our being.

Satan tempted Jesus first at the body level, with food. Jesus was hungry after fasting for 40 days. I would be too. "Let me get you to transgress so you can satisfy your physical needs…" was his first attempt. *This usually works on most people*, he was probably thinking.

Could we be so easily ensnared? By food? Would we really sell our soul for a crust of bread? I'd like to think not, but I may be deceiving myself. Considering the great lengths we'll go to in an attempt to feed our flesh, many of us just need a tasty, attractive or shiny object dangled in front of us to draw us away.

Satan's next try tested Jesus at the soul level. *Will you look to your own soul for answers?* In the verse Satan quoted from Psalm 91, God was clearly not talking about climbing a building and jumping off. Satan was taking God's Word and twisting its intent for his own purposes; to get Jesus to hurl himself off the top peak of the temple to see if angels would catch Him. Not a good plan.

Our souls think we know something. Our souls think they can find the right answers through logic. Our souls think they can even read God's Word and figure out the meaning on their own, relying on its own human wisdom interpretation of the Word. Without the Holy Spirit's guidance as we read the Word, we fall back to our default setting: leaning on our own understanding. Would Jesus fall for it (pun intended)? No, no He didn't.

Satan's last-ditch effort tempted Jesus' spirit. You have power, and who will You serve it with? Who will you worship? Give Your identity away to me and You can have all the kingdoms of the earth. Jesus would have been such a prize catch that Satan offered up *every* earthly kingdom if He would just worship him. You can gain the whole world, but lose your spiritual self to darkness. Jesus knew He had a Kingdom far superior already, and exclaimed, "Away with you, Satan! For it is written, 'You shall worship the Lord your God, and Him only you shall serve.'"

Serve Him only!

Deuteronomy 6, Psalm 91, Matthew 4, Luke 4

7 Lessons of Temptation

After fasting for 40 days, Satan tempted Jesus in the wilderness. Although He was in a physically weakened state by the end, He was spiritually strengthened.

While reading about the temptation of Jesus, seven powerful lessons stood out.

Temptation *can* be overcome.
It is possible to successfully resist temptation! Jesus did, therefore it is our heritage, too. Satan cannot make you fall into sin, so resist him and he will flee.

Answer temptation back with the Word.
Jesus answered every one of Satan's temptations with a scripture in its correct context. Jesus knew the Word and used it, modeling the way for us.

Clearly know your identity
Satan will attempt to sow seeds of doubt in your heart and mind about your true, God-given identity. *"If you are the Son of God..."* Satan cannot take your identity, but through ignorance you can give it away.

Know and rightly divide the Word.
The inner working of the Holy Spirit is required to fully

and correctly perceive God's Word. Without the Spirit, scriptures can be twisted and misinterpreted to be used in vain. Satan tried to use the Word for his own plots when he told Jesus to throw himself down off the pinnacle of the temple.

If Satan tempted Jesus, he'll also tempt us.
If Jesus wasn't excused from temptation, neither will we be!

Jesus has the power to command physical things.
"If you are the Son of God, command these stones to become bread." Satan knew Jesus had the power to command with His words and things would happen in the natural realm. What he didn't know is if Jesus would use His words for His own purposes, disobeying God. Do our words serve ourselves (and our own desires) or God?

Temptation comes at the body, soul and spirit levels.
We will be tempted at every level of our being.

There was one more noteworthy thought that arose. After Jesus' time of fasting and testing, His ministry launched, full force. Is it possible that the spiritual work we're called to won't become mature (when it comes to overcoming temptation) until we are?

Matthew 4
Luke 4

Power Supply

Imagine the river of God overtaking you, carrying you along its path; winding, flowing, refreshing, a gentle strength. See yourself at one with this river, fully connected to its contents; wisdom, peace, love, and life move through your body, naturally. You and the river are one.

On the shore, you notice someone who needs help. You simply stand and walk towards them, the water diverting to remain connected to you. You don't fully understand the person's need, but you don't have to. You know every remedy is found in the Lord. As your mouth opens, the very water that flows through you streams out to them. You are a watercourse for the River of Life.

When God gave me this vision, He was teaching me a new way to interact with Him. Have you heard anyone who serves the Lord saying they need to go "recharge their batteries?" I have. In fact I've said it myself, and I've heard many people teaching about the need to store up spiritual strength in order to serve others without becoming dry inside. After all, we cannot give what we do not possess, right?

It is true...as people, there's no doubt we need rest! Being quiet and alone with God is also biblical. Even

Jesus found secluded time to pray. However, I'm no longer sure that the mindset of needing to "recharge our batteries" is all there is. Although that concept is a step along our spiritual maturity process, it's not the highest level available to us in God.

Seeing how much of the Lord I can store up in order to pour out makes it still about *my* capacity; about what *I* can handle. Fill up the cup, pour it out, repeat. Increase my capacity…now I have a pitcher-sized vessel. Fill up the pitcher, pour it out, repeat. Increase my capacity…to a bucket, etc. It's still about me. God can certainly use me even so, but there has to be more.

Do we want to be tied to the battery backup system, or do we want to be conduits? Like the watercourse, a conduit is a connector; a go-between for power or flow to get from here to there. Is it possible for us to be conduits, spiritually? To live in a constant state of being an open vessel for God to flow through? To live in His presence, letting Him do the work? Yes it is.

Teach us how to walk in the Spirit, Father. Take us from glory to glory as You mature us. Bring the light of Your presence to cleanse us from all unrighteousness so that You have unrestricted flow through us. Amen.

They've Got Nothing

Darkness has very few schemes and devices at their disposal. If you cannot be tempted, intimidated by fear or if you don't believe lies and can't be deceived, darkness has nothing else they can use against you. They've got nothing.

Temptation comes in all shapes and sizes: greed, lust, gluttony, rebellion, pride, violence, theft, addiction, hate, jealously, shrinking back, deception, and lying to name a few. If we recognize temptations as an attempt to derail us, we avoid debilitating soul traps. As we know, Satan will test our weak spots, but Jesus proved overcoming temptation is possible.

Fear and intimidation is darkness' go-to move. If the roar of a scary news story, an attack on your character and reputation or imaginations full of fearful outcomes is all it takes to back you down, their job was easy. Anyone who doesn't understand and use their delegated authority in Christ is an easy target for the tactic of fear. Be strong in the Lord and in His mighty power!

Lies have to do with the power of words. Lies are made to deceive. Some words are subtly deceiving, doubt-inspiring, half-truths, causing you to relinquish your power, to remain in confused insignificance, and to set aside vision. Some lies of darkness want people to think Satan has more to offer than God does. Lies are not only the opposite of truth, they are also seeds for spiritual weeds. Belief systems in our hearts can be seeded by lies leaving no room for the truth to enter in.

By knowing God's Word and His voice and renewing our minds, we will no longer be tricked by lies. We will no longer believe any of darkness' lies are true when the light of God's truth shines within.

In John 14:30, Jesus made the statement that Satan has nothing *in* Him, meaning the kingdom of darkness had zero foothold in His life; no legal right to occupy any space within His heart. He couldn't be tempted, He was not fearful, couldn't be intimidated and saw lies for what they were.

Because of all Jesus has done for us, we each have a huge amount of spiritual power over darkness' ability to affect us. They have **nothing** that we don't allow them to have.

John 14:30

Longing for Perfection

I am not a fan of imperfection. My soul groans at the thought of it. Imperfectness is frustrating. I don't like it in myself, in others or in the world in general.

Injustice is a form of imperfection. Injustice is someone participating with imperfection and perpetuating it, purposefully. Sickness is imperfection; an imperfect body. Cars and houses that break down are imperfect, and so are selfish attitudes and lies that tear us down.

When God made the earth, it started out perfect. No weeds, no sin, no shame, no death, nothing was wrong, whatsoever. When Adam and Eve sinned, the death of perfection happened, immediately.

We were made in God's image, having started in perfection. This is why we long for it still…

Even if the idea of reaching a state of inner spiritual perfection as an individual were possible, the world around us would still continue to be imperfect. Things get rotten, zippers break, people die, dogs poop on carpets, machines break down, temptation comes, and garbage piles up. I cannot obtain perfection in this life.

Imperfection is our current reality. Rather than relentlessly pursuing perfection, it's more profitable that I pursue Christ, Himself. Becoming more and more Christ-like doesn't mean we attain perfection here, but we are, then, able to access more of *His* perfection; more of His ability, resources, character, perspective, heart, and Spirit. A wise woman once told me, "Progress, not perfection."

In Heaven, *nothing* rots and no garbage exists. There is no fear to hold us back. Nothing is broken, and all needs are met. Heaven has more than enough, always. It's a place of wholeness, completion and perfection. My heart longs for this.

A wise man once taught me, "Learn to love imperfection." I'm working on this daily, although now I understand why my heart longs so much for the perfection God originally created.

Father, our imperfections and the imperfections of the world are ever before us. Sometimes we wonder how You can use us and others for Your great works with all our flaws. Thank you for Your grace. Chase all fears related to our imperfection away so we can confidently step out into the plans and calling You have for us. Amen.

Psalm 50:2

He is Everything

"*Mercy and truth have met together; righteousness and peace have kissed.*" –Psalm 85:10

"*Righteousness and justice are the foundation of Your throne; mercy and truth go before Your face.*" –Psalm 89:14

God is everything. Sometimes we miss His fullness. It's easy to view Him from a divided perspective. Either He's the Almighty, coming with fire and lightening, or He is our merciful Father, slow to anger and abounding in love. It's not either/or: it's both. God is everything.

Check out the characteristics and names of God, some of which seem to be opposites of each other:

Lion – Lamb
Rock – Lilly of the Valley
Judge – Lover of My Soul
Living Water – Consuming Fire
Lord – Friend
Justice – Mercy
Almighty – Comforter
Avenger – Peace
Judge – Love
Justice – Forgiveness

All Powerful – Humble
King of Kings – Helper
Most High – Shepherd
Awesome God – Loving-Kindness
Ruler of Heaven – Emmanuel
Mighty One of Israel – Wonderful
Law – Grace
High Priest – Savior
Master – Abba

It's understandable how confusing God can be to those who don't know Him. People we know don't have the capability to be all these things at once, but God does.

Is He Lord of all, or loving-kindness and patience? Yes.
Is He fiercesome, or good? Yes.
Is He powerful, or gentle? Yes.
Is He the Man of Fire, or beautiful? Yes.
Is He God with us, or is He seated in Heaven? Yes.

He is our peace, and He is our strength. He is our Deliverer, and He is our Comforter. He is our Everlasting Father, and He is the Son of Man. He is gracious and full of compassion, and He is to be feared.

Open our eyes, Lord, to see Your fullness. You are our everything.

Habits or Faith?

"...when the Son of Man comes, will He really find faith on the earth?" –Luke 18:8b

Good, godly habits do not equal faith. If I consider myself a person of faith because of my daily habits and lifestyle, I could be in trouble. While good habits are very helpful to have in every aspect of life, they can be completely devoid of faith. They can also become religious rituals.

Jesus wondered if He would find faith on the earth when He returns. Certainly there will be people with godly habits, but that doesn't necessarily mean any faith will be found within them.

Good habits may initially have started because of obedience to God's Word or as an act of faith, but can quickly become auto-pilot actions. "So, Nancy, why do you attend church?" "Well, it's just something my family and I have done for years." "Jim, how wonderful that you pray with your kids at mealtime." "Yeah, we have a special blessing they've memorized." "Dave, you've really cleaned up your language lately. What happened?" "I'm more conscious about not swearing because my new girlfriend doesn't like it."

Those are just a few ultra-simple examples. Is an active faith found in any of those situations? Maybe...but not necessarily.

Faith drives works, but works (that are simply good habits) should not *be* our faith.

Lord, if I take an honest look, where has my faith become stale and lifeless? Where have I settled for meaningless action? Where am I on auto-pilot? Have I created a life so padded that I don't need any faith?

Faith sees the impossible and the invisible, beyond our own strength, knowledge or ability. Faith creates the opportunity to participate in spiritual things. If faith started something, let it also finish it.

Can the spark of faith be rekindled in our habits? Yes. Whether it's giving, honesty, prayer, practicing patience, being loving, volunteering and serving, teaching, walking away from temptation, or whatever you do that is good, remember *why*. Remember and thank the One you're doing it for, and thank Him for giving you the strength and wisdom to do it. Give it fresh power.

I dedicate this action to you, Lord. Keep the awareness of You and Your purposes close to my heart and always on my mind. I desire to have my whole life serve You and Your Kingdom, purposefully. May faith always drive my works.

Hebrews 11:1
James 2

39%

Our thought life is not a private conversation.

The digital readout "39%" flashed in my mind during prayer: a message from God revealing the percentage of my thoughts that are honoring to Him.

I would have thought I was doing better than 39%... apparently not. Each of us has a percentage of negative vs. positive thoughts, and God is very aware of it. God's insights reveal what we need to know so we can change. God shows us a heart issue first, then helps us fix it. Having 61% of my thoughts not be pleasing to Him is definitely an issue.

All negative, fearful, angry, immoral, scheming, selfish, grouchy, condemning, timid, and prideful thoughts dishonor the Lord. Thoughts that meditate on His Word, that are full of faith, that give people a second chance, are forgiving, keep joy and peace, that are humble yet confident, and thoughts that plan and strategize how to be a blessing honor Him.

I felt no condemnation as He showed me 39%. He did not reveal that to me to shame me. In fact, He never reveals err of our hearts to shame or disgrace us; it's always for our awareness; always to move us in the right direction. He graciously shows us our blind spots; blind spots that hold us back from abundant life.

"Let the words of my mouth and the meditation of my heart be acceptable in Your sight, O Lord, my strength and my Redeemer." –Psalm 19:14

May my thoughts be pleasing to You, Father. Show me my blind spots, Lord, then help me change them to match Your ways.

Bad Breath

"I'm only concerned with spiritual bad breath," I heard Him reply as I apologized for the bad breath that went along with my whispered, early morning prayer. Our unholytosis is what concerns Him, not our halitosis.

Halitosis, otherwise known as bad breath, is a problem in which a noticeably unpleasant odor is present with exhaled breath. Unholytosis is the spiritual bad breath we emit when the outflow of our heart is polluted. It's the bad breath exhale from our heart that God smells in the spirit realm.

"...those things which proceed out of the mouth come from the heart, and they defile a man. For out of the heart proceed evil thoughts, murders, adulteries, fornications, thefts, false witness, blasphemies. These are the things that defile a man..." –Matthew 15:18-20a

It reminded me of a different day when I was eating lunch with my Bible and spilled a drip of salad dressing on a page. I quickly wiped it up, feeling a need to respect God's Word and not soil it. *Sorry, Lord. I need to keep this clean...*Immediately I heard, "My Word is clean already."

When it comes to things of a spiritual nature—like people and His Word—God is unconcerned with the physical sight or smell of them. He looks at the heart. He pays very close attention to the condition of hearts.

"For the Lord does not see as man sees; for man looks at the outward appearance, but the Lord looks at the heart."
–1 Samuel 16:7b

"Let my prayer be set before You as incense, the lifting up of my hands as the evening sacrifice." –Psalm 141:2

"For out of the abundance of the heart his mouth speaks."
–Luke 6:45

"I will bless the Lord at all times; His praise shall continually be in my mouth." –Psalm 34:1

Psalm 62:4
Proverbs 15:28
Ezekiel 20:41
Matthew 12:34
Ephesians 5:2

Righteousness

"A good man leaves an inheritance to his children's children, but the wealth of the sinner is stored up for the righteous." –Proverbs 13:22

"For You, O Lord, will bless the righteous; with favor You will surround him as with a shield." –Psalm 5:12

"For the eyes of the Lord are on the righteous, and His ears are open to their prayers..." –1 Peter 3:12

"The voice of rejoicing and salvation is in the tents of the righteous..." –Psalm 118:15

Considering the great rewards presented in these promises, have you ever thought to yourself, *I've gotta get me some righteousness...?* Or, *Lord, I desire to be righteous. Please help me become righteous so I can be pleasing to You.* We become painfully aware of what's missing.

One day however, all the dots connected: we can never *get* righteousness. Our righteousness (the 'goodness' level we can achieve) is as filthy rags (Is. 64:6). We have zero righteousness in and of ourselves, and we can never manufacture it.

"There is none righteous, no, not one," says Paul in Romans chapter 3.

So what can we do? Righteousness isn't something we can *get*, but it is something we can *receive*. Romans 5:17 calls it 'a gift of God' which comes through Jesus. It's a gift that we can 'put on' and participate with.

Follow this trail with me: Genesis 15:6 says, *"Abraham believed God and it was accounted to him as righteousness."*

Romans 3:22 – *"...the righteousness of God [comes], through faith in Jesus Christ, to all and on all who believe."*

2 Corinthians 5:21 – *"For He made Him who knew no sin to be sin for us, that we might become the righteousness of God in Him."*

Isaiah 26:2 says, *"Open the gates, that the righteous nation which keeps the truth may enter in."* I want to be part of this righteous nation that is allowed to enter God's gates. Notice that those who *keep the truth* may enter. Abraham kept the truth because he believed God.

Want to enter? Be righteous. Want righteousness? Believe and keep the truth. There is a 'way of righteousness' and that way is Jesus. He is the way, the truth and the life (John 14:6). When we believe in Jesus, we receive the Holy Spirit *and* the righteousness of God.

God supplies all our needs; even the righteousness He requires!

The Key

Knock, knock.
Who's there?
It's Your child. Can I come in?
Sure! You have a key. Use it.

Having a key means you can let yourself in and out. Having a key is a higher level of trust. Without one, you just have to knock and wait.

At salvation, we receive a seal, a key – the Holy Spirit indwelling within us is the Kingdom key. It gets us in the door. Five of the ten virgins in Matthew 25 had the key, and they were allowed into the wedding.

The key initially opens salvation, like gaining access to the foyer of a mansion. However, your new key won't immediately open *every* door in the place, but it will open some. At work, we may be given a front door key, but that doesn't mean it will open the supply cabinet, the storage room, or the boss' office. Some of us have not been granted access to certain areas (or things) in the Kingdom, yet.

The Lord, Himself, has to upgrade your key and grant you access to other rooms when you're ready; rooms of greater revelation and understanding, greater anointing, experiences, visions, abilities, gifts, mantles, grace, and perspective.

When my Holy Spirit key hasn't opened something that I know is available to me in the Kingdom, I need to knock and wait; seek and ask.

> *"So I say to you, ask, and it will be given to you; seek and you will find; knock, and it will be opened to you."*
> –Luke 11:9

Soul development, filling up with the Word and heart cleansing prepares a person for experiencing the greater glories in the (currently) locked rooms. And, some Kingdom doors can only be opened through praise and worship. Rather than contending and struggling unnecessarily, true worship in spirit and in truth will cause some things to be opened to you with ease.

Kingdom seekers are not satisfied with foyer and hallway access. Allow your hunger for the Kingdom to grow your key's effectiveness; to increase the amount of Holy Spirit and fire that works within you and through you.

> *"They go from strength to strength…"* –Psalm 84:7a

> *"…we all…are being transformed into the same image [of the Lord] from glory to glory…"* –2 Corinthians 3:18

Matthew 7:7, Matthew 16:19, Revelation 3:7

External Viewpoint

What is truly valuable in life? I believe it is eternal things, but do I really walk that out?

Recently, I drove by a local high school just as school was getting out. Lots of kids were milling about, walking, talking, standing, and leaving for home. I contemplated their insecure-looking mannerisms and efforts to 'be somebody' so they'd be accepted and noticed.

Although it was a bunch of teenagers, this scene would have looked much the same had I been driving through a business district, college campus, church parking lot, or mall.

The world tells us these things are what's valuable: pretty hair, having a certain figure or build, being tough, having expensive stuff, achievement, appearance and image, acting cool, puffing up your attitude, etc. It's all focused on the external: stuff, status and appearance.

**We think too much like people and
not enough like God.**

Jesus values the internal state of our lives, and He encourages us to cast aside worldly cares. They choke out true life.

> "...*the cares of this world, the deceitfulness of riches, and the desires for other things entering in choke the word, and it becomes unfruitful.*" –Mark 4:19

His all-seeing eyes can scan a soul searching for valuable assets, such as faith, self-control, kindness, humility, confidence, truth, honesty, purity, diligence, passion, righteousness, wisdom, and vision. His eyes look for spiritual fruit – eternal things.

May our eyes also look for eternal things and esteem them greatly.

Lord, help me to get rid of my external viewpoint. Help me to think more like you and less like people with human wisdom. Give me Your eyes so I can rightly discern, see and under-stand. My great desire is to see like You see. Create in me a pure heart and renew a steadfast spirit within me. Thank you, Lord. In Jesus' name.

Genesis 3:19
Luke 12
Galatians 5

Bondage to Prosperity

"He brings out those who are bound into prosperity."
– Psalm 68:6b

We cannot prosper or increase in the things of God in any area of life in which we are bound. Jesus spoke many times of agricultural processes when He discussed prosperity; fields, seedtime, harvest, soil qualities, and fruit. A field with bondage is restricted and burdened, becoming unfruitful and bare.

What bondages limit our prosperity?

<u>Sameness</u> – expecting different results from the same old actions.
<u>Small minded</u> – small vision or feeling insignificant.
<u>Limiting beliefs</u> – when your belief system tells you that you can't.
<u>Being on the wrong path</u> – when prosperity is set up for me over here, but I'm over there…
<u>Having unhealthy or encumbered heart soil</u> – see Luke 8, the Parable of the Sower.
<u>Hoarding</u> – don't be a rich fool…or a poor fool for that matter.
<u>Missing the season</u> – stick close to the Holy Spirit to discern the seasons. Peas don't grow in December.

<u>Aimless living</u> – aiming for nothing ensures no target is ever hit. Distractions abound.
<u>Disobedience</u> – if God can't partner with something, He certainly can't bless it.
<u>Unforgiveness</u> – unforgiveness is like concrete. It won't move and can't ever grow anything.
<u>Fear</u> – fear-based decisions will always be the wrong decisions.
<u>Inactivity</u> – there's always a good excuse to do nothing.

When it comes to how hoarding limits prosperity, I find this fascinating: how can *giving away* our seed cause *our own* field to produce *more*? In the natural, it makes absolutely no sense. Only God. Our natural mind says *keep it all for myself*, but this is not what the mind of Christ says. Generosity is what's valued and rewarded in His Kingdom.

Feeling like you missed your season of prosperity? Well, guess what? Seasons are cyclical. All God needs is heart soil that's prepped and ready for His Word to enter in to and produce a harvest. Good dirt can't help but be prosperous. Get ready – planting season is coming around again!

Father, help me see the err of my ways. Unfetter me and take me from bondage to prosperity.

Psalm 119:37
Proverbs 20:4
Matthew 6:15
Matthew 13

Illegal Substance

"Now faith is the substance of things hoped for, the evidence of things not seen." –Hebrews 11:1

Faith: a polarizing word. Faith is often rejected and banned from workplaces, schools, family reunions, government offices, Hollywood, and even entire countries.

Is faith an illegal substance?!

Hebrews 11:6 tells us that without faith it is impossible to please God. And in Luke 18:8, Jesus is wondering whether or not He will really find faith on the earth when He returns. Faith may be banned in the world, but it's a BIG deal to God.

"Now faith is the substance..." Faith *is a* substance; a spiritual substance that I believe can be easily discerned in the spirit realm. What does it look like? I'm not sure, but I imagine it existing in our hearts in various amounts, shining like gold.

When we trust and believe God and His Word, we have faith. When we have the substance of faith within our hearts, we become trustworthy in God's sight. And, our faith pleases Him.

> *"But without faith it is impossible to please Him..."*
> –Hebrews 11:6

> *"For the eyes of the Lord run to and fro throughout the whole earth, to show Himself strong on behalf of those whose heart is loyal to Him."* –2 Chronicles 16:9

What do you think His eyes are searching the whole earth *for*? Faith.

Bibles are illegal in certain countries. Possessing one could mean jail or death. Being a Christian—a person of faith—in some areas is dangerous. However, being found without faith in God's sight has even more severe, eternal consequences. If faith is an illegal substance in the world, let me be found enormously guilty!

> *"For whoever desires to save his life will lose it, but whoever loses his life for My sake and the gospel's will save it."*
> –Mark 8:35

Matthew 8:26
John 12:25

Praise Emission

Like faith, praise and worship is a substance in the spirit realm. I've seen it.

While awake with my eyes closed, I saw the church's 500-seat sanctuary full of people. As they all participated boisterously in praise and worship, true expression and spirit and truth worship caused something to emanate from their spirits, upward. Something was happening in the spirit realm. It looked like incense or the smoke from a lit candle.

The rising smoke filled the entire room; wall to wall, corner to corner. There was a pouring out feeling, like a pure exhale with purpose, power and love; a rich offering God would be pleased by.

Suddenly, the vision changed. The sanctuary was still full of people and the music still played on, but rather than wall to wall expression and large amounts of praise substance rising up, only a few, gentle wisps rose here and there. Very few people in the room had any true offering to release to God from their hearts. Very few really understood how to worship.

In a book I once read, someone else shared a vision

about how praise and worship that's poured out of people's hearts is collected and presented to God. The prayers of the saints are also collected, as Revelation 8 describes. "And the smoke of the incense, with the prayers of the saints, ascended before God from the angel's hand." And, since praise and worship is prayer set to music, this makes perfect sense.

Because the emission of praise and worship is a powerful, valuable substance, pursuing God through worshipping Him is vital. My God-given vision showing *'this is what I desire, but this is how it is'* clearly was meant to reveal our deficiency in praise and worship. I, for many years, did not know how to worship or express my heart to God. I literally did not know how. Even today I still have more freedom of expression to develop, but He has worked with me step by step.

Lord, I commit myself to opening my heart to You and giving You the praise You deserve. As I learn to praise You, I start with gratitude and thanking You for all You've done. I move into confirming Your righteousness and goodness, then singing Your Word and Your promises for myself, others and the lost.

Psalm 141:2
John 4:23-24

Keep Your Harvest

"Ha, ha! Now you cannot reproduce! I just stole your efforts!" I victoriously declared after snapping off a dandelion's flower along the gravel path that leads to my sister's house.

No sooner had those words escaped my mouth than the Spirit spoke to me. *The Devil also wants to steal your harvest by clipping off what the Word has grown in your heart.*

Faith and confidence is imperative to hold onto within our hearts. It's like a plant: if you chop off its blossom or bud, all its effort was for nothing. Without the flower, its reproduction, multiplication power and increase is cut off.

"Therefore do not cast away your confidence, which has great reward. For you have need of endurance, so that after you have done the will of God, you may receive the promise."
– Hebrews 10:35-36

We can start off well in believing—having faith and confidence for something God has promised or showed us—but if we don't continue and finish well, doubt and unbelief steals our harvest.

Deer in my yard are also culprits for stealing harvests, when they eat the blossoms off my apple trees in spring. Their ravenous teeth sever and eat what was supposed to be mine at a later date. The tree remains, but its harvest for that season has been cut off. Likewise, doubt comes along like clippers and chops off what we've been believing for.

> *"You did not choose Me, but I chose you and appointed you that you should go and bear fruit, and that **your fruit should remain**, that whatever you ask the Father in My name He may give you."* – John 15:16

The Word grows amazing things within our hearts when we receive it in. Take Him at His Word, fully believing that what He has promised He can also perform, holding on to hope and confidence. Hope and belief must be contended for, otherwise the clippers of doubt steal what the Word started to grow before the harvest comes.

"Why do we abstain from Hope? Often even very seasoned ones in the Body of Christ no longer want to risk hoping. The reason is obvious: we've been let down before over and over, and the best way to save from disappointment is not to have an expectation; not to have a hope on the record. But, guess what? We have to contend for *hope*. Hope is one of the three greats that remain in 1 Corinthians 12 (faith, hope, love)."
–Johnny Enlow

Contend for hope!
Contend for your harvest!

Say Something

"We are so afraid of rejection that we won't show our gifts and talents!"

In a dream, those were the words I heard myself yelling out to a room full of people. In this dream, my pastor had to leave the sanctuary to hide himself. An enemy had come and threatened to harm him, but he found a safe place. When he left, so did many people in the congregation because of fear, but not everyone. Many others stayed. I was left to speak to the dwindling crowd.

An enormous boldness rose up within me, and I spoke with authority to encourage and ignite the boldness of others. My words helped turn the fearful into faithful. Told others of their delegated authority through Christ, and rallied them to step out into boldness, too.

That dream held several lessons.

1. There are many times in life when our pastor isn't there. *We* are the only one there with a Holy Spirit message inside us.

2. Not everyone will want to stay and hear what you

have to say, but some will.

3. One of our greatest fears is rejection. The fear of man is a snare, and snares hold us back.

4. The power of one voice can change situations, mindsets and hearts. So, whenever you have the opportunity to, be bold and use yours.

My husband and I watched a WWII documentary one evening and I had a big revelation. Adolf Hitler started out as a low-ranking soldier for Germany; an unknown person with no political influence. He became so indignant after Germany's defeat in WWI, that his passion for revenge and power led him to speak his mind to any who would listen. At first, most people thought he was weird. Then, as citizens' sentiment grew resentful, people started listening to his rants. Essentially, he gained power by talking. And talking. And yelling. And persuading. And rallying. And talking. A crazy, evil man took control simply because he had something to say with his loud voice.

Just because a loud opinion is shared, doesn't mean there's any truth or wisdom in it.

I burn with the message of *express what God has given you*. If *you* had the chance to speak a powerful message to anyone who would stay and listen, what is the message you have that the people must know? Or, if you yelled a battle cry to rally others, what would it be?

You (yes you) go be a loud voice for good. It's time to say something!

Kingdom Currency

On earth, our currency is money; things like cash, precious metals, coins. We earn money through work, spending our time and effort to get more. Since I know God uses natural things as an example of spiritual things, one day I wondered, "What is the currency of the Kingdom?" Earth currency must represent something spiritual; there had to be a spiritual equivalent.

I've heard people say that faith is the currency of the Kingdom. God has shown me something slightly different. My quest led to this conclusion: the Word is the currency of the Kingdom.

Let's take a look at this. In the natural, we check our bank statement to see how we're doing with our level of currency. But, in our spiritual bank, the equivalent is how much of the Word (wisdom) we have built up.

Here's a strange thought: we don't really need money. What we really need is the end result of what money can get us (food, shelter, clothing, tools, transportation, etc.). Not to sound irreverent, but do we need words and wisdom, in and of themselves? No, but we definitely need what it brings into our lives.

We have to get the Word first (through hearing) before faith. Faith represents the *what we really need*...faith is what causes the increase; the multiplication factor and the fruit producer. The Word is the seed, growing into faith (the proper environment for increase), then produces a harvest in our life.

> *"So then faith comes by hearing, and hearing by the Word of God."* –Romans 10:17

The Word gets us what we really need. Here is a comparison:

Money – we trade it for time (through our efforts), it can be shared with others, we can store it up, sowing it buys everything we want and need.

Word – it takes time and purposeful effort to collect, it can be shared with others, we can store it up, sowing it into our hearts produces amazing things for our lives.

Also, just like money in the bank can sit idle, doing nothing for years, so can the Word that we've collected sit idle in our hearts.

This might sound strange, but we cannot share our faith with others. What? Yes...you cannot reach into yourself, grab a chunk of your faith and share it. However, you can give them some of your Word currency (just like you could give someone money). When we say *I'm sharing my faith*, it really means to give your testimony or share wisdom from the Word with them. Even when we tell our stories we're declaring His goodness, His love, His power, His promises, His wisdom, His provision...we are sharing the Word and how it (He) has impacted our lives. We can share the Word we've stored up.

What's really exciting is that when we share our Kingdom currency, *our* portion never diminishes! When we share natural currency, that bank balance creeps lower and lower, but God does have promises about special provision for tithers and those who support His Kingdom purposes with their currency.

One last thought: since the Word is a seed, money is too. Since your money is a seed in the natural, consider carefully what you sow it into. Whatever we sow into, prospers and increases, whether good or bad.

God, may I be voraciously hungry to obtain more and more Word and share it generously with others, sowing it wisely. Cause the Word seed to greatly increase and produce a harvest that remains through faith.

Proverbs 4:23
Hosea 10:12
Malachi 3:10-11
Matthew 13:23
1 Peter 1:23

Desolate Heritages

"I will preserve You [Jesus] and give You [Jesus] as a covenant to the people, to restore the earth, to cause them to inherit the desolate heritages" –Isaiah 49:8

Sometimes when you read the Bible, your eyes scan a verse or section and you realize *there's something deeper here*. There are times when I get stuck or fixed on one verse for days. Isaiah 49:8 is one of those verses. Two pieces intrigued me.

Restore the earth...restore it to what state or condition? And, **desolate heritages**. What desolate heritages?

According to Yahoo.com's dictionary section, here's what these words individually mean:

Desolate: devoid of inhabitants; deserted; lifeless; forsaken; to rid or deprive of inhabitants; to feel sadness; abandoned.

Heritage: a birthright; property that is or can be inherited; something passed down from preceding generations.

Together, these powerful words paint a picture of

humanity having been given something of worth from God, but forsaking and abandoning it; losing it. In the context of Isaiah 49:8, whatever those desolate heritages are, Jesus came to restore them to us; to *cause* us to inherit them. And, whatever God has for me, I want it.

My question was to God: "So, what *are* these desolate heritages that are ours to inherit?"

From what the verse says, it has to do with the earth being restored and us taking something back. We were separated from something; a birthright. And, my understanding is that sin is what separates us from God (Is. 59:2). Sin separated us from heritages that were ours.

What were we separated from that used to be ours? A direct relationship with God, access to all Kingdom resources, and authority on earth.

God wants to restore His original creation – earth, as an extension of Heaven. What does that look like? Look to Eden:

We have dominion and authority
His presence - the Lord walks with us
Heavenly items and beings are available to us
Bodies free of sickness
No shame
Peace and safety

"For the earnest expectation of the creation waiteth for the revealing [manifestation] of the sons of God." –Romans 8:19

> *"For the creation was subjected to futility, not willingly, but because of Him who subjected it, in hope that the creation itself also will be set free from its slavery to corruption into the freedom of the glory of the children of God…the whole creation groans…"* –Romans 8:20-21

Through His sacrifice and shed blood, Jesus is causing these desolate heritages to be restored to us (or for us to be restored to them).

If something is blocking these promises and heritages from truly being manifested in my life, the problem lies on my end, not His. Jesus has done His restorative work: it is finished.

So, how do we take hold of these heritages? First, we need to understand what is ours. We don't know what we don't know, and we don't want to perish because we lack knowledge. Since we can't believe what we don't have knowledge of, first get the knowledge. Second, we don't earn it, we simply believe and accept it. Sound too simple? It is simple, and the simplicity confounds many. Third, ask God *how* to walk in it; how to *be* the manifestation of that truth/promise. Get His grace and wisdom to walk it out.

Father, help me see and take firm hold of everything You have established for me. In Jesus' name, amen.

Genesis 1-2

Get His Vision

"Is this the scope of vision my people have?"

As I perused my favorite social media site one day, I came across a photo an acquaintance had posted of her "vision board." It had all the typical vision board items: big house, vacation, piles of money, achievements, sports car – every symbol of worldly success you can think of.

I pondered it for a moment, and God spoke to me. *"Is this the scope of vision My people have?"* I knew what He meant by this – He wondered if we have any real vision. Is what's represented on this board, it? Is that all? Does this represent My people's true goal?

Many questions came up for me. As His body, are we seeking first what the world offers or are we truly seeking first His Kingdom and righteousness? Are our pursuits focused on stuff and status or on His plans and purposes? It caused me to examine myself, too.

While it's fine to want upgraded houses, cars and jobs (and God knows I love a good vacation…), making it our life's *vision* isn't. Each of us play a vital role within His plans and purposes, and He gives each of us some of His desires and passions. Ask yourself this important question:

> What piece of His heart for the world and people around you did He give you?

Is it to see no child go hungry?
Is it to touch and heal broken hearts through art?
Is it to pray for and see the sick be healed?
Is it to financially support the Kingdom in a huge way?
Is it to see marriages strong and healthy?
Is it to take the gospel to the nations?

These are the kinds of things God cares about. This is His vision. When our desires match His desires; when we want what He wants...*BOOM!* This is when powerful things happen: doors of opportunity fling open, divine connections are made, provision pours, and we clearly see His hand orchestrating details and circumstances.

> Can we get a new vision: His vision?
> Can we want what He wants?

Father, help my desires and vision to match Yours. Show me the cares, causes and people that you've designed me to love and serve. Your will be done, Lord. I trust in your ability to meet my every need, and I am satisfied by the goodness of Your house. Thank you, Lord.

Matthew 6

The Cross of 'Others'

"When He had called the people to Himself, with His disciples also, He said to them, 'Whoever desires to come after Me, let him deny himself, and take up his cross, and follow Me.'" –Mark 8:34

Without a deep need, we aren't moved. If we didn't have to satisfy our hunger, I suspect some people wouldn't even have a job!

"The person who labors, labors for himself, for his hungry mouth drives him on." –Proverbs 16:26

When it's not our need, we tend to not be moved to take action. However…if it was my child that needed a miracle, how intense would my prayers, praise, fasting and attention be vs. for someone else's child? If my finances were in dire straits and I was on the edge of homelessness, out of desperation, what resourceful actions would I dare take? If it were my job, my health, my marriage…?

Usually, our hearts have to be deeply invested *in* something before we'll get up and *do* something. Information alone rarely provokes movement. Some people view God's Word and His values simply as "information."

If the cross of Jesus had an inscription on it, I believe it would say "OTHERS." His beautiful life was given up for the purpose of reconciling people to God. Jesus didn't need reconciliation Himself – *He* was already one with God. He was complete. But, God had a greater, Kingdom cause on His heart motivating Jesus to act.

Jesus, in essence, *is* God's heart. He sent His son (His heart) into the world so we would understand His heart for us. We needed to see and experience it.

"For God so loved the world that He gave His only begotten Son, that whoever believes in Him should not perish but have everlasting life." –John 3:16

When we lose our lives for His sake, we, also, take up the cross of *others*. We do not carry other people's crosses for them or take up a cross of punishment: we take up *our* cross that is all about our service to others.

Why is having the mind of Christ and the heart of God important? Because then what we love matches what He loves, causing us to spend ourselves for His purposes.

Keep it Simple

Simple appeals to me. Jesus kept it simple. His life was lived for the Kingdom – nothing more, nothing less. His life was uncomplicated, unhindered, unconcerned about the opinions of others or fleshly desires. He couldn't be drawn away from His purpose or distracted by other ideas. He recognized temptations and dismissed them. People had other plans for Him, but He kept moving ahead with God's plan even though it involved pain.

Jesus was the most humble and, at the same time, the most powerful person to ever walk the planet in human flesh. How can someone that powerful be so humble? He kept it simple.

I want to be like Jesus when I grow up!

For me, keeping it simple might look like this:

Clarity about my calling and purpose keeps my eyes focused forward, helping me know what to say yes to, what to say no to, and what direction to move in.

Temptation, distractions and deception are quickly discerned and dismissed.

I could look at a situation, opportunity or relationship and clearly see whether or not getting involved would cause entanglements and a subtraction, or if it was meant to add to my life in a positive way.

Avoid caring about worthless things or getting wrapped up in trends and what's considered "cool" for the moment.

Living a regret-free life, including words I speak, loving others well, being careful about what I allow to enter my eyes, and fearlessly stepping out in faith.

A simple desire to live with clean hands and a pure heart, causing peace to reign in my soul.

Knowing and using the delegated authority and power given to me through Christ.

Not trying to make things happen in my own strength or understanding, but allowing God to direct and work through me at all times.

    I pray that we meet each day with a holy KISS:
keep **i**t **s**imple, **s**aint!

Psalm 24:4
Psalm 119:37
Matthew 28:18-20
Romans 16:16
James 4:8

Disappointments

Can disappointments lead to divine appointments?

"I would have lost heart unless I had believed that I would see the goodness of the Lord in the land of the living. Wait on the Lord, be of good courage and He shall strengthen your heart. Wait, I say, on the Lord." –Psalm 37:13-14

Adversity, struggle, failure, unmet expectation, defeat, set-backs, delay, or derailing can happen in any area of life: relationships, ministry, health, business, finances, and dreams.

A few years ago, a prophetic woman said something to me that I didn't fully grasp at the time. She told me that God had allowed me to experience many disappointments in life in order to mature me.

Disappointments are more subtle adversities. These disappointing circumstances aren't obvious tests of our faith and don't usually appear as in-your-face adversity. A giant doesn't show up at your door. They often mask themselves as irritations, circumstantial injustices, the loss of a hope, dream or potential idea, unanswered prayers, effort leading to naught, or plans that fail. I cannot tell you how many of these I've endured.

We understand that adversity and disappointments have two potential outcomes: either they make us stronger and wiser, or derail us into the ditch. For those of us who don't give up, a new level of strength, faith and courage comes. For those of us who become disillusioned and draw back, stagnation or regression looms.

Winston Churchill had amazing adversity and huge failure in his life. Abraham Lincoln experienced defeat after defeat on his journey to the white house. Both of these men made a choice not to bow to disappointments or adversity. It made them fierce, powerful, wise.

God wants His people to not only *have* an inheritance, but He also wants us to inherit characteristics, such as perseverance, boldness, wisdom, resolve, grace, and surrender. In His perspective, I believe it's more valuable that our faith and trust increases than having a plan succeed.

"Unrelenting disappointment leaves you heartsick, but a sudden good break can turn life around." –Proverbs 13:12

Shift your thoughts and perspective: from now on, view disappointments as adversity meant to mature you. Your divine appointment with destiny and with the calling God has on your life could depend on the maturity level developed through overcoming your disappointments.

Psalm 37

Release Your Words!

"Do not withhold good from those to whom it is due, when it is in the power of your hand to do so." –Proverbs 3:27

Or, when it's in the power of your *mouth* to do so. Sometimes, withholding our words equals withholding a blessing.

Quite frankly though, some words need to *not* be released! We know which types those are...angry, cursing, degrading, false, gripes and complaints, gossip, and inappropriate ones, to name a few. Those are the kinds of damaging words to hold back.

However, God has shown me I tend to hold back good words, too; words that would bless and encourage others, words that could build up, words that could break chains, words that can change the spiritual atmosphere, healing words, words that could cause God's hand to move and His resources to come.

Some words cause the Kingdom to advance.

In the Old Testament, conferring a blessing to someone was completely comprised of *words*.

> "Then God appeared to Jacob again, when he came from Padan Aram, and blessed him." –Genesis 35:9

> "By faith Jacob, when he was dying, blessed each of the sons of Joseph, and worshiped, leaning on the top of his staff."
> –Hebrews 11:21

If God's words are so powerful they can command a universe to form, and *we* are made in His image, our words are also a powerful, creative force. Release your words!

What can you create today?

Who can you bless today?

What situation can you command today?

> "Let the **words** of my **mouth** and the meditation of my heart be acceptable in Your sight, O Lord, my strength and my Redeemer." –Psalm 19:14

Deuteronomy 28:8
Psalm 133:3
Proverbs 15:23
Proverbs 25:11
Luke 4:36
Acts 4:31

Survival Mode

People are so bogged down by sin, selfishness, stress and distraction that often, loving others well gets pushed aside for 'survival.' In the United States, we really are *surviving* quite well materially, but because of being over-burdened and out of focus, we can't always see that. What we do see, however, is all the worldly requirements necessary to *be somebody*, and all the striving we have to do to get there.

Survival mode takes our eyes off the Kingdom...and the King. Like Peter, when he stepped out of the boat to walk on the Sea of Galilee to Jesus, when he looked away at all the turmoil all around him, his soul reverted to survival mode. *"And when Peter had come down out of the boat, he walked on the water to go to Jesus. But when he saw that the wind was boisterous, he was afraid; and beginning to sink he cried out, saying, 'Lord, save me!'"* (Matt. 14:29-30)

Peter bravely got out of the boat—more than can be said for the other 11 disciples who stayed in and watched—and I believe he would have been successful in reaching Jesus if only his eyes had maintained staring at Jesus.

There were two realities at that moment: Jesus, the

reality of the Kingdom come, and the physical world. Get a picture of that scene in your mind. See Jesus with arm outstretched, waiting. Put yourself in Peter's (wet) shoes. See the two contradicting realities: The reality of Jesus and His power vs. the reality of the wind and waves. Jesus overcame the world, in every way.

Our eyes have options. Those same two realities are happening right now. Do you see it? Understanding this revelation will be life-changing.

Peter reverted to a typical human response in a time of fear and stress: survival mode. Notice the differences in living in a mode of love vs. survival:

Love Mode	vs.	Survival Mode
Peaceful		Frantic
Contentment		Fearful
Flow		Scarcity
Outward Focus		Striving
Confidence		Worry
Freedom to 'Be'		Limitations
Giving		Taking
Vision		Competition
Purpose		Confusion
Eternal Eye		Physical Eye

"...for the kingdom of God is...righteousness and peace and joy in the Holy Spirit." –Romans 14:17

Where is my life and focus? On the earth, in survival mode, waiting for Heaven? Or, is it looking and living in the reality of the Kingdom, now?

Matthew 6

Kingdom Increase

"Of the increase of His government and peace there will be no end" – Isaiah 9:7a

God LOVES increase. He's always on the lookout for increase. In fact, He requires it of His servants. Read Matthew 25's Parable of the Talents. The call for all the Master's servants to increase is undeniable.

The parable tells the story of a master who left money for his servants to steward while he was away. Two servants took his instructions to heart and got a "Well done, good and faithful servant" response. A third was fearful, doing nothing with his lot, and received a severe rebuke.

Is the idea of Kingdom increase all about money? In this parable, the talents were money, but that's only one small piece to the larger, Kingdom increase puzzle.

Profitable (profit), fruitful (fruit), productive (produce), prosperous (prosper), abundant (abundance), enlarge, growth, harvest, multiply, gain, overflow…these *increase* words are found repeatedly in the Bible.

Think about eating food: we either maintain, increase

or decrease our physical body's mass according to our eating habits. It's the same with our souls. Our souls consume every day. Whatever is coming in through our eyes and ears (books, movies, news, TV, music, conversations, games, etc.) feeds our spiritual selves, causing a maintenance of wherever we've been, an increased fatness of soul or a shrinkage - an emaciation (depending on what we're *eating* – health or trash).

Physically, being thin and fit is best. However, spiritually, having a fatness of soul is extremely valuable. I want to be *very* spiritually fat.

Another word for fat is *prosperous*...Joseph prospered even during injustices and dire circumstances. Why? Because the Lord was with him. In Psalm 118, King David cries out, "I pray, send now prosperity." He might as well have said, "Send now Jesus!" Jesus *is* prosperity. Pursuing Jesus is the increase X factor.

And then there's the Rich Fool from Luke 12 who had an enormous increase happen on his farm. But, he had three main problems:

1. He thought the overflow was for him.
2. He thought he had "arrived" and his work was done.
3. His focus was not on Kingdom increase.

These are examples of where God wants to see increase in our lives, on the earth and in His Kingdom:

Strength	Power
Joy	Dominion
Peace	Family/Children

Believers	Faith
Kingdom Come	Gifts
Tents	Anointing
Territory/Land	Knowledge
Good	Understanding
Word/Seed Growth	Wisdom
Provision	Giving
Salvation	Love

"The kingdom of heaven is like leaven [yeast], which a woman took and hid in three measures of meal till it was all leavened." –Matthew 13:33

The Lord wants the Kingdom to increase within you. The Lord wants the Kingdom to expand out and encompass more and more people. He also wants it to have increased influence and dominion on the earth. The Kingdom is meant to increase, in every way.

Kingdom increase is what Jesus' is watching for. "Who can produce increase? I will give them more…"

"For to everyone who has, more will be given, and he will have abundance; but from him who does not have, even what he has will be taken away. And cast the unprofitable servant into the outer darkness…" –Matthew 25:29-30a

"May the Lord give you increase more and more, you and your children." –Psalm 115.14

Deuteronomy 7:13
Isaiah 51:2, Matthew 25
Romans 3:12, Titus 3:9

Wind, Fire and Oil

*"The **wind** blows where it wishes, and you hear the sound of it, but cannot tell where it comes from and where it goes. So is everyone who is born of the Spirit."* –John 3:8

*"He will baptize you with the Holy Spirit and **fire**."* –Matthew 3:11 and Luke 3:16

*"And you shall take the anointing **oil**, and anoint the tabernacle and all that is in it; and you shall hallow it and all its utensils, and it shall be holy."* –Exodus 40:9

In the Bible, the Holy Spirit is frequently symbolized by wind, fire and oil.

Wind (Hebrew: *Ruach*) – the way in which He moves, comes and goes, His presence, the breath of life.
Fire (Hebrew: *Aish*) – the way in which He empowers, purifies, tests, consumes, enters, cleanses, speaks.
Oil (Hebrew: *Shemen ha-mishchah*) – the way in which He blesses, rests upon, sanctifies and consecrates, chooses, heals, marks, anoints.

*"And the Lord God formed man of the dust of the ground, and breathed into his nostrils the **breath of life** [wind]; and man became a living being."* –Genesis 2:7

Without the wind, or breath of God, we cannot live. He gave us our spirit by breathing life into us. On Pentecost, He did part two of His infilling. The Holy Spirit traveled from Heaven to the upper room where the disciples were gathered, filling their spirits with Himself. You have your own spirit and God's Spirit within your physical body.

> *"And suddenly there came a sound from heaven, as of a rushing mighty **wind**, and it filled the whole house where they were sitting. Then there appeared to them divided tongues, as of **fire**, and one sat upon each of them."*
> –Acts 2:2-3

The Lord ignites us with His holy fire.

> *"…His word was in mine heart like a burning **fire** shut up in my bones…"* –Jeremiah 20:9

He also warns us about the dangers of unholy fire.

> *"And Nadab and Abihu, the sons of Aaron, each took his censer and put fire in it, and put incense on it, and offered strange and unholy fire before the Lord, as He had not commanded them."* –Leviticus 10:1

> *"Can a man take fire to his bosom, and his clothes not be burned? Can one walk on hot coals, and his feet not be seared?"* –Proverbs 6:27-28

Burning with ungodly desires has consequences. If we take ungodly fire into our laps, expect to be burned by it! If we take Holy Spirit fire into our heart, expect to be refined!

Oil was required for the lamp in the tabernacle's holy place. Without oil, the lamp (the light) would go dark.

> *"Command the children of Israel that they bring to you pure **oil** of pressed olives for the light, to make the lamps burn continually."* –Leviticus 24:2

> *"Then Samuel took the horn of **oil** and anointed him in the midst of his brothers; and the Spirit of the Lord came upon David from that day forward."* –1 Samuel 16:13

> *"Those who were foolish took their lamps and took no **oil** with them, but the wise took oil in their vessels with their lamps."* –Matthew 25:3-4

We are to have oil in our vessels. The oil marks the spot and provides the fuel for where the fire is to burn. Oil also marks the spot where healing needs to come. Just as the blood of the lamb marked the children of Israel's doors in Egypt at the first Pentecost, the oil marks what belongs to God. "This belongs to Me."

> *"And they cast out many demons, and anointed with **oil** many who were sick, and healed them."* –Mark 6:13

> *"Is anyone among you sick? Let him call for the elders of the church, and let them pray over him, anointing him with **oil** in the name of the Lord."* –James 5:14

Thank you, Father, for Your wind, fire and oil of the Holy Spirit! We welcome them into our vessels.

Hands and Mouths

"Thus I will bless You while I live; I will lift up my hands in Your name." –Psalm 63:4

"I will bless the Lord at all times; His praise shall continually be in my mouth." –Psalm 34:1

Hands and mouths are two of our most powerful, physical tools in the natural; tools that also have spiritual implications. Hands and mouths can bless the Lord and others. Both can also *harm* the Lord's work and others.

"...who may stand in His holy place? He who has clean hands and a pure heart, who has not lifted up his soul to an idol, nor sworn deceitfully." –Psalm 24:3-4

We know from Proverbs 4:23 (keep your heart with all diligence...) and John 7:38 (out of your heart will flow rivers of living water...) that our hearts have an outflow, and that outflow proceeds out of our mouths and hands. The evidence of what was in our heart can be seen and heard by what our hands do and what our mouth says.

Allow your hands and mouth to bless the Lord by bringing Him an offering. When our hands are yielded to God, they can give an offering of praise and worship, and so can our mouths. They can also give an offering of trust through tithing or serving, and mouths can pray and give thanks to God.

The second way our hands and mouths can be used is to impact others...hopefully in a positive way! Did you know that hands have the densest concentration of nerve endings in our bodies? Hands can do amazing things: touch, work, comfort, create, express, fix, write, etc. The outflow of our heart causes our hands to move in whatever way the outflow directs.

Mouths contain tongues; one of our body's strongest muscles (actually consisting of 8 cohesive muscles). Mouths, like hands, are directed by our hearts.

The Bible says Jesus' mouth is like a sharp sword several times. "He had in His right hand seven stars, out of His mouth went a sharp two-edged sword" (Rev. 1:16). Hebrews 4:12 and Ephesians 6:17 both call the Word of God a powerful sword we can use. Our mouth becomes a weapon of warfare for the Kingdom, but never to be wielded against people. Our fight is not with people.

Our hands and mouths were never created to harm. Choose to dedicate your mouth and hands to Him, and see what powerful things are accomplished.

"Out of the same mouth proceed blessing and cursing. My brethren, these things ought not to be so." –James 3:10

Ephesians 6

Lord, I'm Distressed

Me: "Lord, my heart is troubled by all the injustice, evil and pain in the world.

Jesus: "It should be, but let not your heart BE troubled. Focus on Me. Let troubling things spur you on to love."

"My heart is angry when people make bad, evil decisions against Your commandments and when things are not as they should be."

"How do you know they're not as they should be?"

"We fall so short of Your glory and it upsets me to see that."

"People fall short to different degrees. Your job is to raise up and teach them to fall less and less short as a part of their process. Don't sin in your anger. Taking anger out on a person is sin."

"What do I do with my anger, Lord?"

"Baptize the anger so it's cooled, washed and rises up as something else; something useful, for My purposes and use, depending on the situation. Sometimes people are in error and get angry when they're confronted with the truth (like the money-changers whose tables I overturned in the temple). That is the anger of pride."

"Jesus, how do You/did You love people who just used You for what You could do for them temporarily but didn't want Your true help?"

"I don't love them for what they can do for Me or based on their behavior. That would be selfish love. I just love them."

"That's hard...I want to know how to do that."

"Start with your family."

Legal System

"For unto us a Child is born, unto us a Son is given; and the government will be upon His shoulder. And His name will be called Wonderful, Counselor, Mighty God, Everlasting Father, Prince of Peace." –Isaiah 9:6

Governments have a legal system as a part of their structure. The Kingdom of God is form of government; a spiritual government that we are citizens of. The spirit realm has a legal system with laws and parameters.

Take note of this common, legal terminology:

Court room	Convicted
Witness	Pardon
Sentencing	Guilty
Judge	Truth
Justice	Mediator
Records	Confession
Accuser	Testimony

Do these sound familiar to you? They're applicable here on earth and in the spirit realm.

At the fall of man, something with legal ramifications

happened: Adam and Eve's participation with sin caused the kingdom of darkness to legally have access to people and earth. Satan suddenly had a legal claim

"The soul who sins shall die." –Ezekiel 18:20a

Luke 12:57-59 warns us to settle with our adversary before getting to the judge. The accuser of the brethren, Satan, is the adversary.

As a witness, your testimony of Jesus and the confession of His work on the cross pays the price for your sin. Your pardon is then sealed in Heaven's courtroom. The government of the spirit realm is on Jesus' shoulders, and we have a legal right to an everlasting inheritance by believing in Him and confessing it with our mouths.

We can't be a witness without having a testimony!

"...Jesus Christ, the faithful witness, the firstborn from the dead, and the ruler over the kings of the earth. To Him who loved us and washed us from our sins in His own blood, and has made us kings and priests to His God and Father, to Him be glory and dominion forever and ever. Amen."
–Revelation 1:5-6

Although we are guilty, God of justice <u>and</u> mercy, thank you for taking our punishment and making a way for us to go free!

Leviticus 4
Hebrews 10

Strongholds

"For though we walk in the flesh, we do not war according to the flesh. For the weapons of our warfare are not carnal but mighty in God for pulling down strongholds..."
–2 Corinthians 10:3-4

Why do Christians still struggle with addiction?
Why are Christians still having affairs?
Why are God's people sick?
Why do I still have fears and ungodly thoughts I can't seem to get rid of?

Have you ever wished all sin and temptation would immediately be removed at salvation? I sure have. Funny how that doesn't happen though. I've heard testimonies of people who've been saved and never took a drink again, although they'd been alcoholics, or others who experienced a physical healing of some sort at salvation. Most of the time, however, an unseen change takes place and struggles remain. Even so, these struggles begin to feel different, and we become more acutely aware of our sin. Part of the Holy Spirit's job is to convict us of sin.

Why do we continue to sin? Stronghold spirits (unclean spirits) are still in operation because of our habits, our woundedness, and the snares that have caught us.

Just as the Holy Spirit has fruit (as described in Galatians 5), stronghold spirits also have fruit (outward evidence of their existence). At first, this was a very hard teaching to accept. I have unclean spirits at work in *my* life? Seriously? After my old belief system and pride were cracked, it was an obvious, missing piece to the puzzle. It made perfect sense and explained a lot. Just as unforgiveness blocks God from working in certain areas of our hearts, strongholds do the same.

Here are just a few examples of unclean, stronghold spirits that the Bible mentions (there are more):

Lying spirit: 1 Kings 22, 2 Chronicles 18
Perverse spirit: Isaiah 19:14
Haughty spirit: Proverbs 16:18
Spirit of fear: 2 Timothy 1:7
Spirit of bondage: Romans 8:15
Spirit of heaviness: Isaiah 61:3
Deaf and dumb spirit: Mark 9:25
Spirit of infirmity: Luke 13:11

Here's what some of their fruit looks like:
Lying: lies, cursing
Perverse: sexual sins
Haughty: greed, selfishness
Fear: terror, anxiety
Bondage: addictions
Heaviness: depression
Deaf and Dumb: mental illness, deafness
Infirmity: sickness and diseases

When God introduces a surprising new idea or layer of truth, He wants to build upon it, but He can't if we don't accept it. When I processed this through with God, and finally got over my embarrassment about still having layers of darkness to evict, it was empowering.

God does not reveal areas we need to change to shame us – only to make us aware so a renewal can take place. We cannot change what we're not aware of, nor will we recognize His help and solution when it comes.

The Holy Spirit is at the center of our spiritual hearts, but that doesn't mean everything else unclean immediately leaves. Because of the legal, spiritual access sin opens within us for darkness to reside, our hearts need a spiritual house cleaning. Once strongholds are identified (and they can be by their fruit), we can command the strongholds to leave.

Thank God for His Holy Spirit, by Whom we can go from glory to glory, becoming more and more filled with light as we walk with Him. Darkness is driven out piece by piece by the light of His presence. It is His desire that we have complete freedom.

Isaiah 61
Romans 6

Recommended reading:
Beyond Fearless: Removing Every Hindrance from Your Life, by Ericka D. Jackson.

Quotes and Thoughts

Before salvation, the Lord pursued us. After salvation, we spend the rest of our lives pursuing Him.

You, Holy Spirit filled Kingdom person, are the place where Heaven touches earth.

"We have got to hear God or we will be deceived."
–Glenda Jackson

Jesus, Himself, prays for you by name.

Whatever we sow into, we increase.

Valuable treasures rarely lay exposed in your path. Treasures of every kind — physical and spiritual — must be hunted for, mined and unearthed.

"There's always enough, because He died." –Heidi Baker

"…the supernatural realm of the Holy Spirit is our inheritance." –Kathie Walters

The adversary lies; sometimes using a person's voice.

About the Author

Krista Dunk is an author, speaker and the project director and co-owner of a publishing company called Creative Force Press. Krista's first book, *Step Out and Take Your Place*, published in 2011, helps people of God discover their God-given gifts and calling by taking a journey to seek Him.

As a child and young adult who struggled with timidity, Krista now finds herself speaking and training in front of audiences large and small. She has also been called to worship as a vocalist and use her American Sign Language skills to inspire others to worship in creative ways; to worship with sign.

Krista and Chris, her husband of 21+ years, live in Washington State with their two children.

Learn more at:
www.KristaDunk.com
www.CreativeForcePress.com
www.StepOutandTakeYourPlace.com

Kingdom Seeker's Devotional is proudly published by:

Creative Force Press
Guiding Aspiring Authors to Release Their Dream

www.CreativeForcePress.com

Do You Have a Book in You?

www.ingramcontent.com/pod-product-compliance
Lightning Source LLC
LaVergne TN
LVHW041342080426
835512LV00006B/574